S0-BFD-349

ANIMAL ATTACK

KILLER SHARKS

Alex Woolf

ARCTURUS

This edition first published in 2011 by Arcturus Publishing

Distributed by Black Rabbit Books
P.O. Box 3263
Mankato
Minnesota MN 56002

Copyright © 2011 Arcturus Publishing Limited

Printed in China

All rights reserved.

Library of Congress Cataloging-in-Publication Data

Woolf, Alex, 1964-
  Killer sharks / Alex Woolf.
      p. cm. -- (Animal attack)
  Includes index.
  ISBN 978-1-84837-948-0 (library binding)
  1. Sharks--Juvenile literature. 2. Dangerous fishes--Juvenile literature. I. Title.
  QL638.9.W67 2012
  597.3--dc22
                                    2011006625

The right of Alex Woolf to be identified as the author of this work has been asserted by him in accordance with the
Copyright, Designs and Patents Act 1988.

Series concept: Alex Woolf
Editor and picture researcher: Alex Woolf
Designer: Ian Winton
Cover designer: Peter Ridley

Picture credits
Corbis: 4 (Denis Scott), 6 (Ralph Clevenger), 10 (Tim Davis), 18 (Amos Nachoum), 19 (Norbert Wu/Science
Faction), 27 (Norbert Wu/Science Faction), 28 (Norbert Wu/Science Faction).
Halasz, Peter: 29.
Kubina, Jeff: 22.
Kühn, Stefan: 11.
Nature Picture Library: cover (Doug Perrine), 8 (Tony Heald), 12 (Michael Pitts), 25 (David Fleetham).
Shutterstock: 5 *top* (BW Folsom), 7 (kbrowne41), 13 (Undersea Discoveries), 15 (Gelia), 16 (cbpix),
17 (Fiona Ayerst), 21 *main picture* (tonobalaguerf), 23 (Christophe Rouziou), 24 (Mark Doherty).
Spotty11222: 21 *inset*.

Every attempt has been made to clear copyright. Should there be any inadvertent omission, please apply to the
publisher for rectification.

Supplier 03, Date 0411, Print Run 1043
SL001709US

Contents

Scary Sharks

Blue water, white death: the great white shark is quite possibly the scariest creature in the sea!

Few creatures can induce fear like the sleek, deadly hunter of the ocean—the shark. Its speed, powerful jaws, and razor-sharp teeth combine to make it one of nature's most lethal killers.

SNACK ON THIS!

Sharks are fish, and belong to the same family as rays and skates. Their skeletons are made of cartilage, not bone.

Sharks have torpedo-shaped bodies and powerful tails that propel them at speeds of up to 30 miles per hour. They also have a superb sense of smell, and can scent blood in the water from miles away. They possess additional senses to detect the tiny vibrations and deep sounds made by their prey.

(Above) Shark teeth are perfectly adapted for eating meat. This tooth, from a great white, has serrated edges—ideal for cutting through flesh and bone.

The ultimate shark movie cliché: a dorsal fin knifes through the water toward unsuspecting swimmers. In fact, it is rare for sharks to swim in this way, except in very shallow water.

Shark facts

- **Prey:** Fish, seals, dolphins, squid, turtles, seabirds
- **Tools:** Speed, strength, teeth, sense of smell
- **Hunting methods:** Solo hunting, search and pursuit, surprise attacks

Great White Shark

Despite their name, great whites are gray on top. This camouflages them in deep water, allowing them to surprise their prey from below.

Legendary star of the movie *Jaws*, the great white is the most famous, and the most feared, of all sharks. Its black eyes, streamlined body, and terrifying teeth are, for many people, the stuff of nightmares.

Great whites are found in almost all the world's seas and oceans. Because they can keep their body temperature higher than the surrounding water, they can survive in very cold seas.

SNACK ON THIS!

The biggest recorded great white was caught in Cuban waters in 1945. It was an incredible 21 feet long and weighed 3.5 tons.

Great whites are responsible for the majority of recorded attacks on humans. This may be because they mistake surfers and divers for prey. It may also be because they are curious creatures and like to test out unfamiliar objects by biting them!

Unusually for sharks, great whites can raise their heads above the water—useful for checking out seals basking on rocks.

Great white facts

- **How long?** 11-16 ft.
- **How heavy?** 1,500-2,400 lb.
- **How dangerous?** Highly! 451 recorded attacks on humans since 1580

More About Great Whites

A great white shark devours a seal off South Africa.

Great white sharks eat seals, otters, seabirds, fish, dolphins, squid, turtles, and even other sharks. They are stealth hunters, who tend to surprise their prey by swimming at them fast from below.

SNACK ON THIS!

Great whites are one of a few species of shark that cannot pump water through their gills to get oxygen. This means they must keep moving all the time, or they will suffocate.

Small seals are struck in mid-body and often tossed clear out of the water, or else grabbed from the surface and pulled down. Large seals are bitten and left to bleed to death.

Like other sharks, great whites have an extra sense that allows them to detect the faint electrical pulses animals emit when they move. Great whites are so sensitive, they can detect another creature's heartbeat.

Great whites have about 3,000 teeth arranged in rows. When the front teeth get broken or worn, the next row of teeth moves forward to take their place.

CHEW ON THAT!

Great whites occasionally attack boats. In 1936, a great white leapt into a South African fishing boat, knocking a crewman into the sea.

Tiger Shark

As their name suggests, tiger sharks are fierce and aggressive predators. They are commonly found in the warm shallow waters of the tropics, but are equally happy in the ocean depths or murky river estuaries.

SNACK ON THIS!

The largest recorded tiger shark was a female caught in 1957. She was 24 ft. long and weighed 3.4 tons.

The tiger shark has a wide mouth and a blunt nose. Its long fins give it lift as it moves through the water.

Tiger sharks have a varied diet. They are generally happy to eat whatever's around, including seabirds, sea snakes, seals, mollusks, crustaceans, fish, squid, and whale carcasses. Thanks to their sharp, serrated teeth, they can even eat hard-shelled creatures such as turtles.

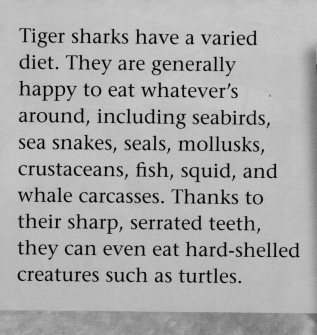

Tiger shark facts

- **How big?** 10-14 ft.
- **How heavy?** 850-1,500 lb.
- **How dangerous?** Second only to great whites–158 recorded attacks on humans since 1580

The tiger shark's teeth are ideal for tearing, piercing, and sawing through the hard skin and shells of their prey.

More About Tiger Sharks

The tiger shark is not a fussy eater. In fact, it is known as "the garbage can of the sea." Their stomachs have been found to contain the strangest things, including number plates, rubber tires and bottles.

Tiger sharks are so named because when they are young their skin is covered with tigerlike stripes and spots. These fade as they mature.

Tiger sharks have also been known to eat gas cans, alarm clocks, baseballs, boat cushions, hubcaps, raincoats, handbags, a suit of armor and a pair of running shoes (with legs still attached!).

SNACK ON THIS!

Some unexpected animal parts have shown up in tiger shark stomachs, including cow hooves, deer antlers, a crocodile's head, a horse's head, cats, pigs, and chickens!

Tiger sharks like warm, coastal waters and this brings them into frequent contact with humans. Their big appetite and aggressive nature can make them a danger to divers and swimmers.

CHEW ON THAT!

In 1935, a tiger shark, introduced to an Australian aquarium, vomited up a human arm. The person the arm belonged to was identified by a tattoo.

A tiger shark in a shallow, tropical sea.

Bull Shark

The bull shark is named for its short, stout body and fierce reputation. It is found in all the world's warmer seas and oceans from Australia to South America.

The shark has poor eyesight, and its hunting technique is known as "bump and bite"—it headbutts its prey to work out what it is, before sinking its teeth into it. So if a bull shark bumps into you while you're swimming, watch out!

Bull shark facts

- **How big?** 7.5-11 ft.
- **How heavy?** 210-600 lb.
- **How dangerous?** Third most dangerous shark–120 recorded attacks on humans since 1580

The bull shark hunts in murky waters where vision isn't much use anyway, and its prey can't see it coming.

Alone among sharks, bulls can swim in both salt water and fresh water, and are often seen in rivers and lakes. In fact, bull sharks have been reported hundreds of miles up the Amazon and Mississippi rivers.

When in fresh water, bull sharks have been known to dine on birds, sloths, dogs, rats, cows, antelopes, horses, and hippos!

SNACK ON THIS!

Bull sharks can tolerate fresh water by reducing the amount of salt and urea in their bodies. They do this by peeing a lot—roughly 20 times as much as when they're in the ocean!

The bull shark's mouth is crammed with hundreds of sharp, pointed teeth.

Gray Reef Shark

Gray reef sharks haunt the shallow, coastal reefs and lagoons of the Indian and Pacific Oceans.

They are aggressive and territorial, often chasing other sharks away from reefs they regard as their own.

The gray reef shark is a fast-moving, agile predator, expert at capturing prey in the open sea.

SNACK ON THIS!

When about to attack, the gray reef shark performs a threat display, raising its snout, dropping its fins, and arching its back while swimming in side-to-side motion.

When a large quantity of food comes their way, these sharks can be provoked into a feeding frenzy. So ferocious are these frenzies that they have been known to eat their fellow sharks in the chaos.

Lemon Shark

The lemon shark gets its name from the yellowish brown coloring of its back. It frequents the warmer coastal waters of the Atlantic and Pacific, and is often seen in bays, docks and river mouths.

Lemon shark facts

- **How big?** 8-10 ft.
- **How heavy?** Up to 400 lb.
- **How dangerous?** 22 recorded attacks since 1580

Lemon sharks have very poor eyesight. They make up for this with powerful sensors in their nose that can pick up the electrical pulses of their prey.

Blue Shark

With its long snout and sleek, torpedo-shaped body, the blue shark can cut through the water at very high speeds, especially when chasing down prey.

Blue sharks are superb long-distance swimmers, and have been known to swim thousands of miles in just a few months. They have been found off the coasts of every continent except Antarctica.

SNACK ON THIS!

The blue shark is the most widely dispersed animal on the planet. It is found in all the world's seas and oceans, from Scandinavia to the tip of South America.

Blue shark facts

- **How big?** 12.5 ft.
- **How heavy?** 300-400 lb.
- **How dangerous?** 41 recorded attacks on humans since 1580

Blue sharks often travel in groups, and are known as the "wolves of the sea." They eat small fish, octopus, lobster, shrimp, and crab. Whale and porpoise meat have also been found in blue shark stomachs, but their favorite food is squid.

When hunting, blue sharks rely on speed. They jet through a group of squid with their jaws open, eating as many as they can.

A blue shark, off the coast of California, gobbles its latest catch.

19

Shortfin Mako Shark

The shortfin mako takes the prize for fastest swimmer in the shark world. It can reach an astonishing 44 miles per hour, over short bursts, and can jump up to 30 feet into the air.

The shortfin mako's streamlined shape and frictionless scales help make it one of the fastest predators in the sea.

SNACK ON THIS!

The shortfin can use its speed to launch itself into the air, and sometimes even land on boats. There have been 20 recorded shortfin attacks on boats. In one case, a mako's bite sank a boat in three minutes!

Because of their super speed, shortfin makos can chase down some extremely fast prey, including tuna, swordfish, sailfish, and other sharks.

The shortfin mako hunts by soaring vertically from beneath its prey and tearing chunks from the victim's sides and fins. Their favourite prey is swordfish—but they don't always come off best in these encounters. Some makos have been found with swordfish bills embedded in their head and gills.

Shortfin mako facts

- **How big?** 6-10 ft.
- **How heavy?** 130-800 lb.
- **How dangerous?** 45 attacks since 1580

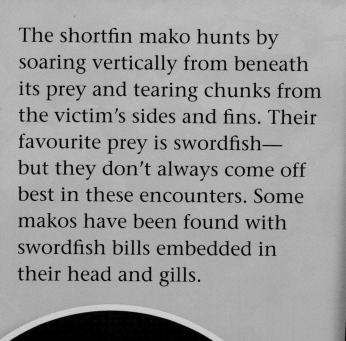

The teeth of the shortfin mako are long, slender and slightly curved. They are visible even when the shark's mouth is closed.

The swordfish—delicious yet dangerous prey of the shortfin mako shark.

Sand Tiger Shark

Sand tiger sharks, also known as gray nurse sharks, are found in sandy coastal waters, shallow reefs, bays, and estuaries. They feed on bony fishes, rays, squids, crabs, lobsters, and other sharks.

Sand tiger sharks appear very fierce with their huge mouth crammed with sharp, curving teeth. In South Africa, they are known as ragged-toothed sharks, or "raggies."

They often hunt in groups, herding fish into tight schools so they can be more easily eaten. Aggressive and usually hungry, they are fed constantly in aquariums to stop them from eating the other fish in the tank!

SNACK ON THIS!

Sand tiger sharks can adjust buoyancy by gulping air and then burping as they swim.

Leopard Shark

This long, slender shark is immediately recognizable by the leopardlike markings on its back. Large groups of leopard sharks are a common sight in the bays, reefs, and estuaries of North America's Pacific coast.

The leopard shark has a remarkable way of eating. It pushes its jaws forward and forms its mouth into a tube through which it sucks up its prey.

CHEW ON THAT!

The leopard shark's mouth has enough suction power to rip a clam out of its shell or suck a worm out of its burrow.

Leopard sharks are "bottom feeders," eating worms, mollusks, and crustaceans off the seabed.

Oceanic Whitetip Shark

The whitetip has a stocky body and long, widely spaced, white-tipped fins.

This solitary, slow-moving deep-ocean shark has been called the most dangerous of all the sharks. This is because it is usually the first on the scene when a boat sinks or a plane crashes into the sea. In fact, it has almost certainly attacked more humans than all other sharks combined.

SNACK ON THIS!

The whitetip was probably responsible for the deaths of many of the 800 who died when the steamship *Nova Scotia* sank off South Africa in 1942.

Oceanic whitetip facts

- **How big?** 6 ft.
- **How heavy?** 370 lb.
- **How dangerous?** Very! Only nine officially recorded attacks since 1580, but has probably killed hundreds

The whitetip likes to eat rays, bony fish, sea turtles, crustaceans, dolphin and whale carcasses, and even trash dumped by humans. Its usual feeding method is to swim into a group of fish with an open mouth in order to eat as many as it can.

The whitetip can become more aggressive when competing with other species for a large food source, such as a whale carcass. This often results in a feeding frenzy.

A whitetip chomps on its latest meal—a triggerfish.

Hammerhead Shark

One of the most unusual-looking of all the sharks is the hammerhead. Its eyes and nostrils are spaced wide apart, giving it a T-shaped head.

The hammerhead's jaws are smaller than most sharks' and can't open as wide. Its mouth is full of small, sharp teeth.

There are, in fact, nine types of hammerhead, of which only one—the bonnethead—is considered dangerous to people. But there have only been 41 recorded hammerhead attacks on humans since 1580.

SNACK ON THIS!

Hammerheads are one of the few animals that can get a tan from being in the sun.

Why the hammer-shaped head? Some scientists say it guides the shark up and down; others that they use it as a way of pinning down stingrays—a favorite meal—to the seafloor. Most likely, the head shape helps them hunt: the electric sensors in their heads are spread out over a broader area.

Hammerhead facts

- **How big?** 5-16 ft.
- **How heavy?** 180-800 lb.
- **How dangerous?** 41 recorded attacks on humans since 1580

No one knows why scalloped hammerheads hang out in groups. It can't be for protection, as they have no predators. Perhaps they just enjoy the company!

Cookiecutter Shark

The cookiecutter is a strange-looking shark found in the warmer waters of the Atlantic and Pacific. It is often called a cigar fish because of its slender brown body.

The cookie-cutter is small—just 20 inches long. It spends most of its time in deep sea at around 11,500 feet, but comes closer to the surface at night to feed.

SNACK ON THIS!

The cookiecutter is bioluminescent: its body glows. It also swallows its own teeth when they wear out–for extra calcium!

The cookiecutter's feeding habits are as bizarre as its appearance. It clamps its teeth on the sides of whales, dolphins, and other sharks and rips chunks of flesh out of them. This doesn't kill them, but leaves them with small, perfectly round, cookie-shaped wounds.

Goblin Shark

The goblin shark has a beaklike snout and a long pair of jaws below that, lined with sharp teeth. It's also pink, due to the blood vessels beneath its semitransparent skin.

The shark lives and hunts in the ocean depths where there's little light. It detects its prey with electric sensors in its snout. When it finds something it likes, such as a deep-sea rockfish, it pushes out its jaws and uses its tongue to suck the victim into its mouth.

The weird-looking goblin shark was first discovered in 1897 when a Japanese fisherman caught one.

CHEW ON THAT!

Around 25 percent of a goblin shark's weight can be its liver, which it uses for buoyancy.

Glossary

agile Able to move quickly and easily.

bioluminescent (of living organisms) Able to emit light.

bottom feeder Marine animals that feed on or near the bottom of a body of water.

buoyancy The ability to float in water.

calcium A soft gray metal that is an essential component of bone, teeth, and shells.

camouflage An animal's natural coloring or form that enables it to blend in with its surroundings.

carcass The dead body of an animal.

cartilage Stiff yet flexible tissue found in the bodies of many animals.

clam A type of marine mollusk.

crustacean A large family of mainly aquatic animals, including crabs, lobsters, shrimps, and barnacles.

dispersed Spread over a wide area.

estuary The mouth of a large river, where it meets the ocean.

feeding frenzy An aggressive and competitive group attack on prey by sharks or other marine predators.

gill The organ a fish uses for breathing.

lagoon A stretch of salt water separated from the sea by a low sandbank or coral reef.

mollusk A large family of invertebrate (spineless) animals that includes snails, slugs, mussels, and octopuses.

predator An animal that preys on other animals.

prey An animal that is hunted and killed by another animal for food.

ray A broad, flat marine animal with large, winglike fins and a long slender tail.

reef A ridge of rock, coral, or sand just above or below the surface of the sea.

sensor An organ or device that detects things.

serrated Having a jagged edge.

shoal A large number of fish swimming together.

skate A large fish of the ray family with a flattened diamond-shaped body.

sloth A slow-moving tropical American mammal.

stealth Cautious, quiet movement.

stingray A bottom-dwelling ray with a flattened diamond-shaped body and a long, poisonous, serrated spine at the base of the tail.

territorial Defending a territory or area.

threat display A form of behavior exhibited by some animals that is intended to scare away a potential enemy.

urea A chemical that forms as a result of the breakdown of protein in the body, and which is excreted in urine.

Further Information

Books

Eye Wonder: Shark by DK Publishing (DK Publishing Inc., 2009)

Face to Face With Sharks by Jennifer Hayes and David Doubilet (National Geographic, 2009)

Shark Life: True Stories About Sharks and the Sea by Peter Benchley and Karen Wojtyla (Random House Children, 2011)

Sharks by Valerie Bodden (Saunders, 2011)

Sharkpedia by Nancy Ellwood (DK Publishing, 2008)

Xtreme Predators: Sharks by S.L. Hamilton (ABDO Publishing, 2010)

Web Sites

animals.howstuffworks.com/fish/shark7.htm
Explains how sharks live, swim, hunt, and eat.

www.bbc.co.uk/nature/class/Chondrichthyes
All about sharks and related species, including some spectacular footage.

www.flmnh.ufl.edu/fish/sharks/Statistics/species2.htm
The International Shark Attack File: all the stats in this book for shark attacks on humans come from this fascinating list.

killersharks.net/sharkfacts
Includes information on the more dangerous species of shark.

www.yourdiscovery.com/web/sharks
General information about sharks, plus specific details about some well-known species.

Index

EDS

DATE DUE		
APR 23 2012		
APR 24 2012		
MAY 02 2012		
5-7-12		
MAY 15 2012		
NOV 02 2012